COME SUNDAY

COME SUNDAY

Photographs by Thomas Roma

Essay by Henry Louis Gates, Jr.

The Museum of Modern Art, New York

Published in conjunction with the exhibition *Come Sunday: Photographs by Thomas Roma*,
organized by John Szarkowski, Director Emeritus, Department of Photography,
The Museum of Modern Art, New York, April 4 to June 18, 1996.

The publication is made possible by a generous grant from CameraWorks, Inc.

Produced by the Department of Publications
The Museum of Modern Art, New York
Osa Brown, Director of Publications
Edited by Christopher Lyon
Designed by Sisco & Evans, New York
Production by Marc Sapir
Halftone photography by Robert J. Hennessey, Middletown, Connecticut
Printed by Meridian Printing, East Greenwich, Rhode Island
Bound by Acme Bookbinding Company, Inc., Charlestown, Massachusetts

Library of Congress Catalogue Card Number 95-82057
ISBN 0-87070-122-3 (clothbound, MoMA, T&H)
ISBN 0-87070-123-1 (paperbound, MoMA)
ISBN 0-8109-6157-1 (clothbound, Abrams)

Clothbound edition distributed in the United States and Canada by Harry N. Abrams, Inc.,
New York, A Times Mirror Company

Clothbound edition distributed outside the United States and Canada by
Thames and Hudson Ltd., London

Printed in the United States of America

The photographs are gelatin-silver prints in the collection of the artist.

Come Sunday

Lord, dear Lord of love
God almighty, God above
Please look down
And see my people through.

Lord, dear Lord of love
God almighty, God above
Please look down
And see my people through.

The lilies of the valley
They'll neither toil nor spin
Come Sunday, oh, come Sunday
That's the day.

I believe the sun and moon
Will range up in the sky
When the clouds are gray
I know it's just clouds passing by.

Up from dawn 'til sunset
Men work hard all the day;
Come Sunday, oh, come Sunday
That's the day.

TRADITIONAL

5

. . . molded on Africa's anvil, tempered down home.

—Julian Bond

We have as much right biblically and otherwise to believe that God is a Negro,
as you buckra, or white, people have to believe that God is a fine looking, symmetrical
and ornamented white man. For the bulk of you . . . believe that God is [a] white-
skinned, blue-eyed, straight-haired, projecting-nosed, compressed-lipped,
and finely-robed *white* gentleman, sitting upon a throne somewhere in the heavens.
Every race of people since time began who have attempted to describe their God by
words, or by paintings, or by carvings, or by any other form or figure, have conveyed
the idea that the God who made them and shaped their destinies was symbolized
in themselves, and why should not the Negro believe that he resembles God
as much so as other people?

—Henry McNeal Turner, editorial in The Voice of Missions,
February 1898

The Church

by Henry Louis Gates, Jr.

WE CALLED IT "The Church." Just "The Church." Baptist or Methodist, A.M.E. or A.M.E Zion, Presbyterian or Pentecostal, Church of God in Christ or Congregational, Seventh Day Adventist or Jehovah's Witnesses—despite all their myriad and microscopic doctrinal differences, in this sense they were all the same, they were just "The Church": African American Christian houses of worship jammed into inner city communities, from storefronts to grand structures that once housed white congregations, from Greek Orthodox and Roman Catholic to Jewish. (The great African American scholar W. E. B. Du Bois once quipped that there were more churches per block in Harlem than in any other comparable geographical area.)

And whether salvation lay in foot washing or full immersion baptism, in communion once a month in sanctified shot glasses filled with Welch's grape juice and embedded in a silver circular tray like eggs in a cardboard carton, or weekly from a silver chalice filled with Christian Brothers wine (a combination, it seemed to me, of Kool-Aid and Cold Duck)—and the narcissism of these minor differences notwithstanding (to paraphrase Freud)—it was, for us, quite simply, "The Church."

Booker T. Washington once claimed, humorously, that "When you meet an American Negro who's not Methodist or a Baptist, some white man's been tampering with his religion," but in fact the number of black Christian denominations is legion. The distinguished black theologian Dr. Benjamin Mays famously said that eleven o'clock on Sunday morning was the most segregated hour in America. I think that Dr. Mays might be astonished to learn, some thirty years after the passage of the Voting Rights Act, that eleven o'clock on Sunday morning remains one of America's most segregated hours—not because of *de jure* segregation, rather because the Church is at once a culture and a black cultural event, a weekly unfolding of ritual and theater, oratory and spectacle, the most sublime music, and even dance.

If the poet Amiri Baraka was accurate when he wrote, "In America, black is a country," then it is also the case that the Church is that country's capital; it's the prime communal ritual ground, the site where the community both consolidates and renews itself. In the Civil Rights movement, the implicit relation between culture and politics, which had obtained since slavery, emerged from underground, and it became an explicit aspect of that political struggle for rights. As Maya Angelou put it so well, the ritual arena for the Civil Rights movement of the sixties was the Church itself, with all of its attendant connotations: "When it came to action," she wrote in 1981, "we were in the church where we had been baptized. We knew when to moan, when to shout, and when to start speaking in tongues." One of the most curious ironies of the post–Civil Rights era of the 1980s and 1990s is that many middle-class blacks find themselves commuting on Sunday from integrated neighborhoods in historically white suburbs *back* to the black inner city churches in which they were raised.

In 1941 the novelist Richard Wright observed, "The church is the door through which we first walked into Western civilization; religion is the form in which America first allowed our personalities to be expressed." It was a *cultural* personality that emerged, one *sui generis*, no longer African but most certainly like nothing else of European descent to be found on this continent. Through the Church, Africans in the New World forged "a common spiritual, economic, and political experience," the author and educator Charles R. Johnson recently argued, and as early as 1940 Ralph Bunche had concluded that the Church "tended to stimulate the sentiments of racial solidarity." "The church, among black people, has been a social cosmos," Kelly Miller, the pioneering Howard University sociology professor, maintained in 1908. "It has provided an emotional outlet, a veritable safety valve for people caught up in the whirling storms of life."

Thomas Roma's photographs capture the sublimity of the beliefs of people who are most "caught up in the whirling storms of life" today, working-class black people for whom the cultural, or ritual, aspects of Sunday worship are secondary at best; no, these are people who believe in a living God, in manifestations of His Spirit, in the power of the Word. They live by faith and believe that faith will be rewarded with eternal life. Roma's worshippers are figures of transcendence, paradoxically all-too-rooted in this world by the burdens of unemployment and underemployment, ghetto housing, and crime-infested neighborhoods.

These are the faithful who "fall out" in the Spirit; if the Holy Ghost is anywhere to be found on a Sunday morning, it is in these churches, among congregants for whom the worship service climaxes in the visitation of the Holy Ghost, manifested by possession, by the Holy Dance, and by the Speaking in Tongues. God and His religion unveil themselves in these holy spaces. And even if a blue-eyed, blond Jesus haunts these storefront walls, the Holy Spirit shows up weekly in blackface, in the fullest range of the resonant thinkers of the African American voice, embodying absolute fear and terror, but also absolute joy. The black church, come Sunday, is where the sublime and the uncanny meet. Sheer joy. As James Baldwin, himself once a born-again child preacher, put it, "To be with God is really to be involved with some enormous, overwhelming desire, and joy, and power which you cannot control, which controls you. God is a means of liberation and not a means to control others."

The Church, certainly, has been criticized by black intellectuals as a conservative force and as an agent of control, otherworldly-directed. As the theologian James Cone put it in 1969, "Unfortunately Christianity came to the black man through white oppressors who demanded that he reject his concern for the world as well as his blackness and affirm the next world and whiteness." Or, as the historian Carter G. Woodson argued in 1945, Christianity too often was the metaphysical counterpart of colonial oppression, "an adjunct of the armed-to-the-teeth Nordic exploiters … carrying out God's will to dispossess others and to exterminate them by segregation." The South African critic Ezekiel Mphalele, writing of his experiences in America in 1959, echoed these sentiments, arguing that too often the Church evaded "the necessity and responsibility of group action. And while it fixed its eyes on Calvary or kept up an aloofness from political realities, the road has been slipping back under its feet."

The Church has been criticized as a conservative cultural force as well, at least since Fats Waller admitted, "They stopped me from swinging in church, so I had to swing outside." And, as the writer Dan Aldridge stated so very well, there is a larger, shared concern about the often artificial distinction within African American culture between the sacred and the profane: "Every Sunday, black congregations sing and perform the music of slave masters and the captains of slave ships while ignoring the music of Ellington, Monk, Coltrane, Tyner, Johnson, Shorter, Byrd, Mingus, Roach, McKinney, and hundreds of others." Yet no one can deny the fundamental shaping role of the Church in African American cultural, social, and political institutions, sacred and secular. The distance between gospel and the blues, the spirituals and jazz, is the distance between Saturday night and Sunday morning. The two most pregnant moments in the African American cultural week, as it were, occur within twelve hours of each other. How could the tones and timbres of the sacred not *but* be informed by the echoes and resonances of the secular the night before? And thank the Lord for it! The Janus faces of black culture are connected by the dawn, come Sunday. Ralph Ellison understood this when he pointed out that "Duke [Ellington was] an example of the mysterious way in which God showed His face in music." I'll never forget the day that I saw Miss Maggie Walker doing the Holy Dance, looking just like James Brown doing the Camel Walk in drag.

I only go to Church occasionally these days. But that was not always the case. When I go today to a black church, it is to experience a certain ritual regeneration, a spiritual renewal through a cultural symbolic crossroads of the arts and belief, of faith and performance, of lyrical utterance and the dance, of metaphor and myth, of tradition and the uncanny. That's why I go to Church now.

When I went as a boy, I went because I believed in God, I believed in Hell,
I believed that the world was coming to an end *soon*, and I believed in the *immediate* transforming
power of prayer to persuade God to intervene in human affairs, whether to calm nerves before
a junior high school dramatic performance, to "get a hundred" on an examination, or to cure my
Mother from a terminal depression.

I joined the Church to fulfill my part of a bargain with God: if He in His
infinite Goodness would just let my Momma come home from the hospital, I would Give My Life to
Christ. He did, three days or so later; and so did I, for the next two years. For the next two years,
I neither smoked nor danced, played cards nor attended movies; I didn't cuss, and Lord knows
I didn't lust in my heart . . . except when I couldn't help it.

Even then, for us Methodists, the truly and deeply religious, the truly holy,
those in *direct* touch with God attended what we called "Holiness" churches, the sort of church
services depicted in this marvelous photographic essay. If the Holy Ghost came to Earth come
Sunday, it visited these churches first and last, to be sure. Worshippers here were not "half steppin'."
They were the true keepers of the Faith, the faith of the early martyrs. And often they had been
martyrs, martyred by an economic system in which enormous odds had been historically stacked
against them, from slavery and racism to unequal access to the tools of literacy and education—
unequal access to hope. And it was hope and its concomitant, courage, that they found in Church,
come Sunday; hope, and an affirmation of their spiritual and cultural selves, in a collective act
of worship and celebration that glorified both God and human will.

I have seen this collective act unfold, I have experienced its reenactment
in the magical prose of James Baldwin and Maya Angelou, Zora Neale Hurston and Toni Morrison,
Ralph Ellison and Alice Walker. But never have I seen it captured more graphically, in more
loving, abundant detail, than in the eight shades of gray that Thomas Roma has exploited on these

pages of photographic paper, in addition to the densest, most somber blacks and the starkest, blinding whites—a feat always difficult, technically, to achieve. If it is true that God is in the details, then Roma has shown us God's many guises—from jeri-curled or corn-rowed hair textures and the subtlest renderings of the vast array of "black" skin tones, to the myriad ways that human eyes record the stages of transformation in the ritual process, in which God becomes Spirit embodying, possessing, only the truly righteous; from creases on newly-pressed suits to wrinkles on the most elegant Sunday dresses. Gesture and movement, faith and belief, silence and dance, rapture and ecstasy, commitment and hope, the sublime immersion in the vale of tears—all of the signal elements of the black dance of religion Thomas Roma has captured in these works of art that are as timeless as is the passion of spiritual transcendence itself. Roma's is a triumph of metaphysical empathy, frozen dynamically in black-and-white.

PLATES

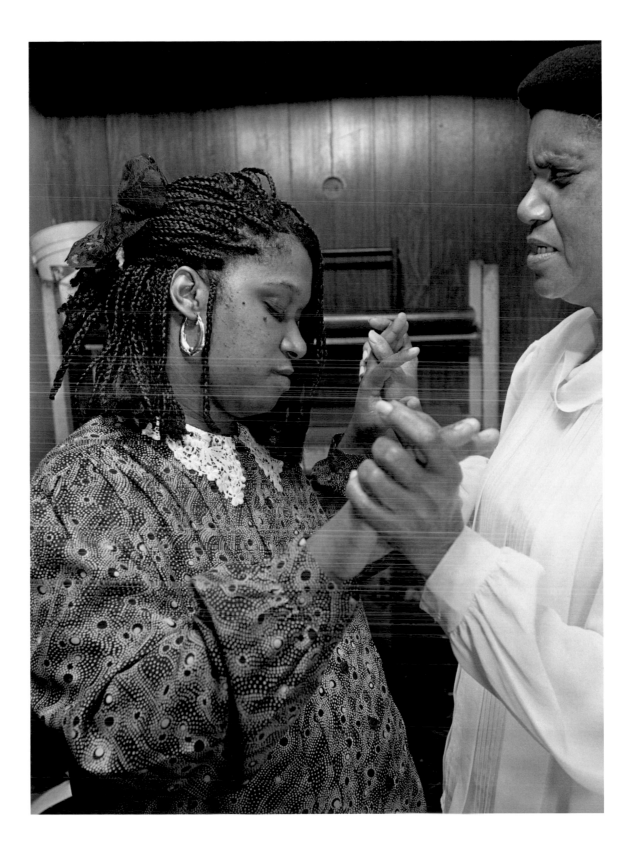

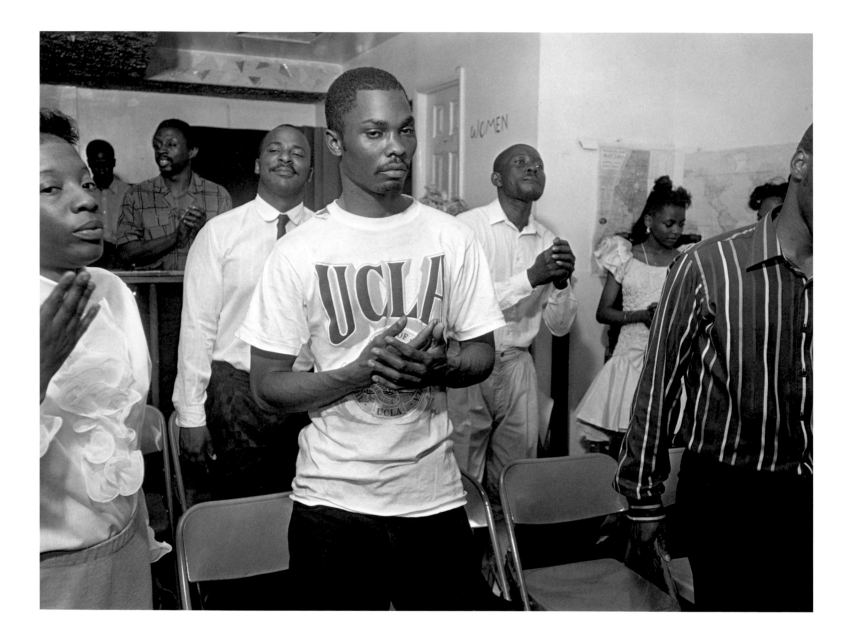

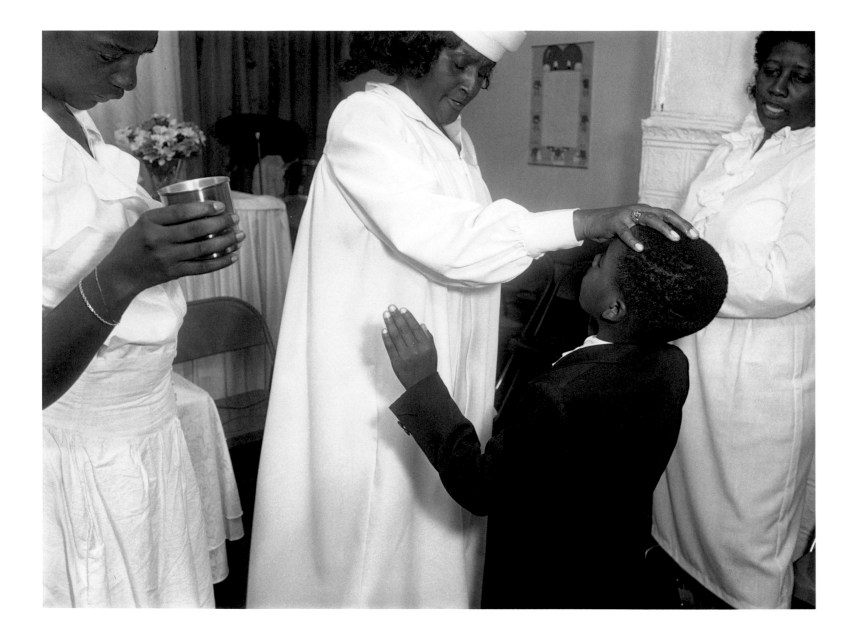

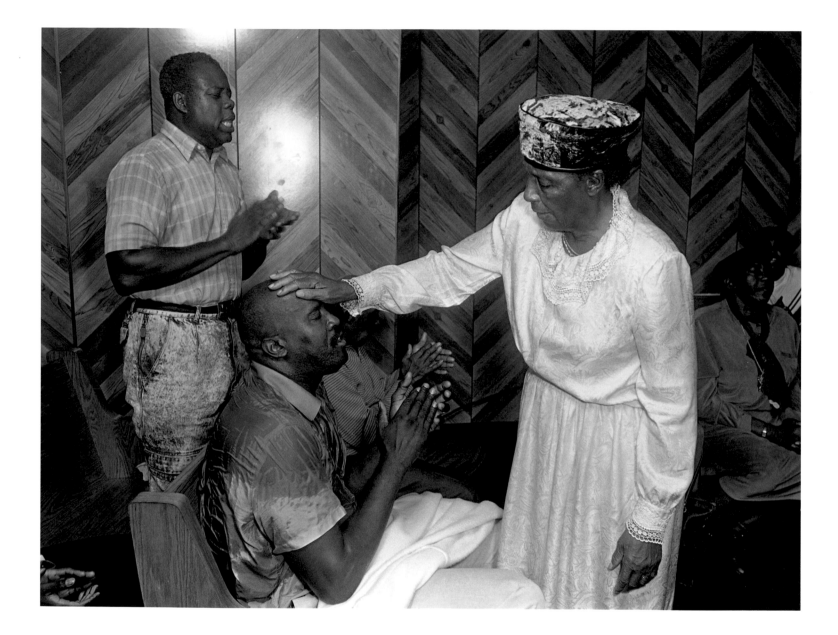

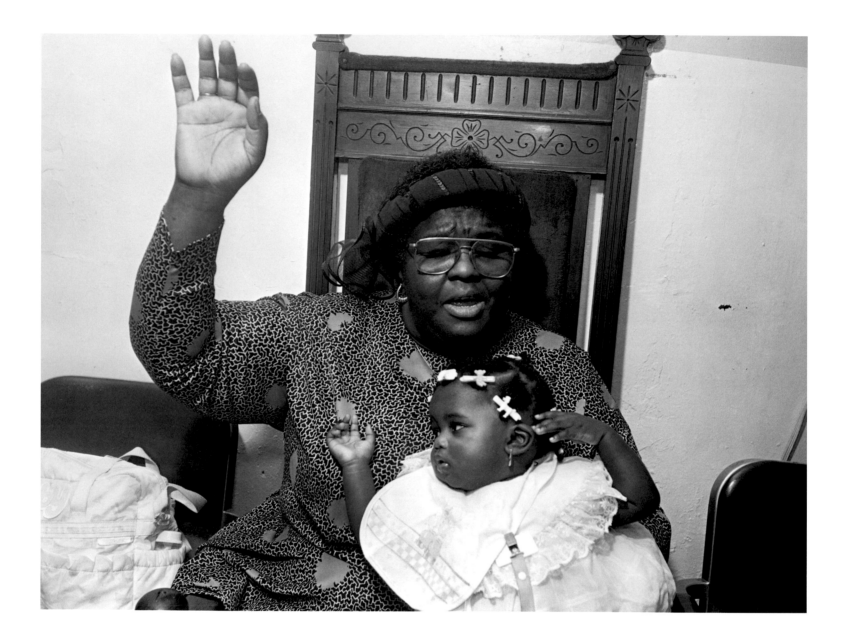

70

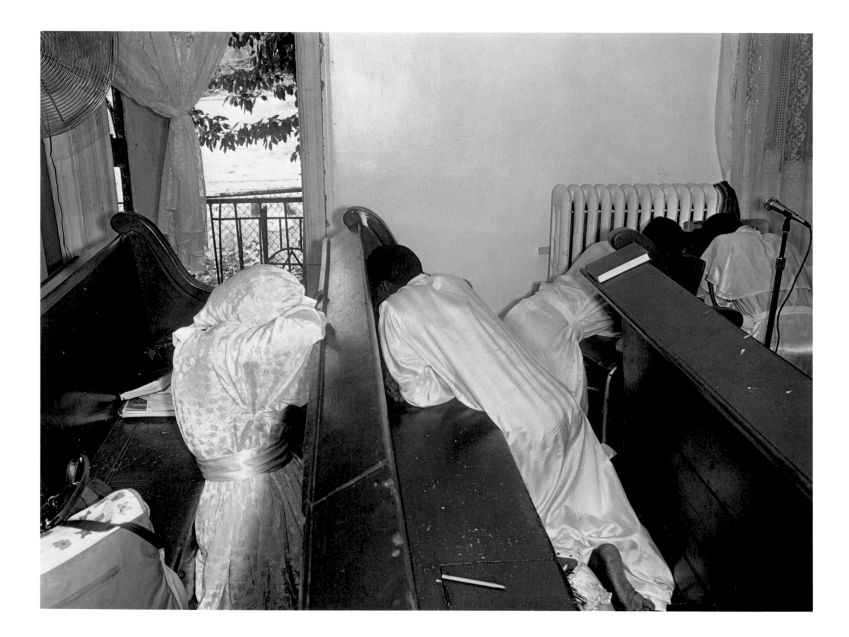

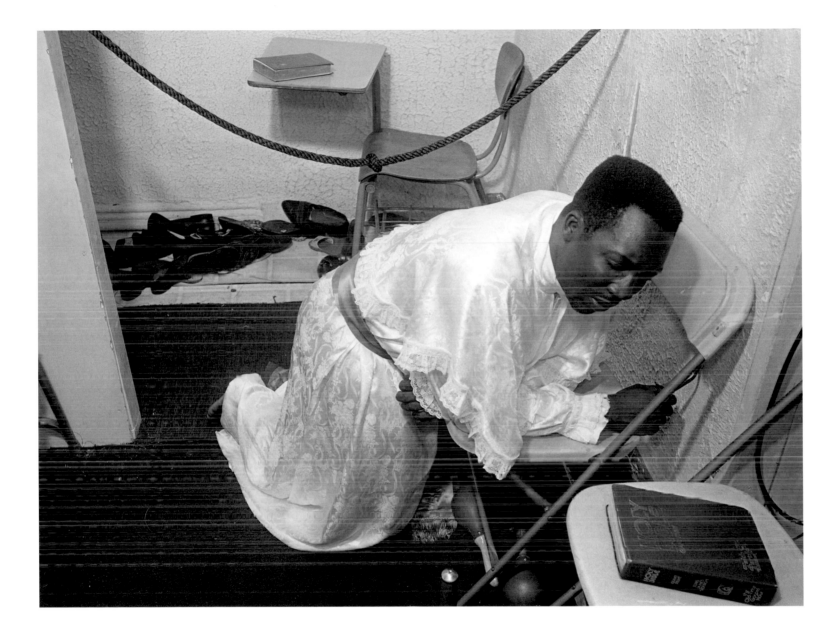

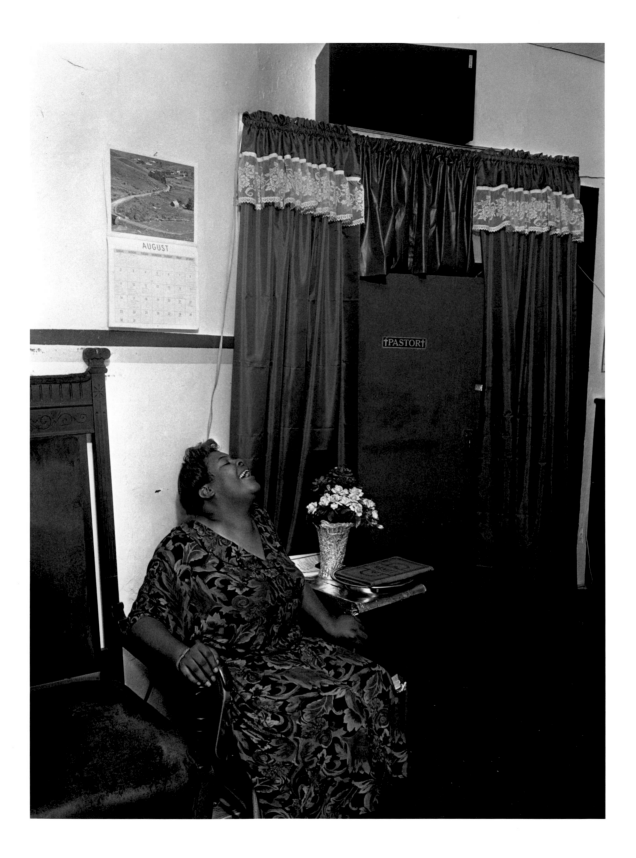

Afterword

Thomas Roma, born in 1950, always has lived in Brooklyn, New York, and has made most of his photographs there. In January 1990 he began a project of photographing houses of worship in Brooklyn, once called the "City of Churches." He planned to include all religious denominations and, eventually, to assemble his photographs in a book titled *God's Work*.

One day in the summer of 1991, in the East New York section of Brooklyn, Roma was preparing to make a picture of a former Jewish temple that had been converted to serve a black Christian congregation. Encountering the pastor of the church, the photographer explained his project. The pastor responded, "The truth is—and you should know better—that God's work is not the building itself but what goes on inside." He invited Roma to return the following Sunday to photograph the service itself.

That invitation decisively changed Roma's project. Over the next three years he photographed more than one hundred and fifty services in African-American Christian churches in Brooklyn. In all, Roma made pictures in fifty-two churches—a year of Sundays. *Come Sunday* presents a selection of those pictures.

The eighty-seven photographs have been selected from a much larger body of work and sequenced for this book by John Szarkowski, Director Emeritus, Department of Photography. Mr. Szarkowski also has organized the exhibition presented by the Museum in conjunction with the publication of the book. I am grateful to him and to Henry Louis Gates, Jr., for the spirited and thoughtful essay that completes the book. The book has been made possible by a generous grant from CameraWorks, Inc.

Peter Galassi
Chief Curator, Department of Photography

Photographer's Acknowledgments

I wish to dedicate this book to all the pastors and congregations who had faith in what I was trying to do, and who, with open hearts, set aside differences of doctrine, nationality, and race, and invited me in.

I want to thank Peter Galassi, for his belief in my pictures and for his commitment to exhibit and publish them, and John Szarkowski, for his sensitive editing and sequencing. I am grateful for the care and concern they both have shown for my work.

I would also like to thank Lee Friedlander, Susan Kismaric, and Raghubir Singh for their support and encouragement while the work was in progress. I am deeply in debt to Jenny Olsson for all she has done since the pictures were taken, working with me on every aspect of the project to see it through to conclusion.

I want to express my gratitude to Howard Stein, for his understanding of what the project could mean and for his generous support, and to the John Simon Guggenheim Memorial Foundation for the fellowship that enabled me to begin it.

Lastly, a special thanks to my wife Anna Roma, without whose faith and patience this work could not have been done.

Thomas Roma

Trustees of The Museum of Modern Art